This title was originally cataloged by the Library of Congress as follows:
Cerf, Bennett Alfred. Book of riddles. Illustrated by Roy McKie. New York, Beginner Books; distributed by Random House, © 1960. 62 p. illus. 24 cm. (Beginner books, B-15) 1. Riddles.   PN6371.C35
793.735   60-13492   ISBN: 0-394-80015-X (trade); 0-394-90015-4 (lib. bdg.)

Manufactured in the United States of America

Bennett Cerf's
Book of
Riddles

Illustrated by Roy Mc Kie

BEGINNER BOOKS
A Division of Random House, Inc.

Why do birds fly south?

Because it is too far to walk.

What gets lost every time you stand up?

Your lap.

What kind of dog has no tail?

A hot dog.

What is the last thing you
take off when you go to bed?

You take your feet off the
floor.

What do giraffes have that
no other animals have?

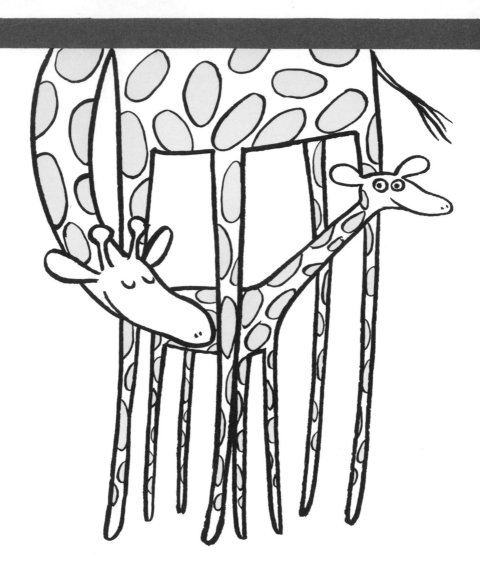

Little giraffes.

Why does the fireman wear
red suspenders?

To keep his pants up.

Why did the little boy throw
the clock out the window?

Because he wanted to see
time fly.

What is the best way to
make a fire with two sticks?

Make sure one of the sticks
is a match.

What time is it when an elephant sits on a fence?

Time to get a new fence.

What did the big firecracker
say to the little firecracker?

"My pop is bigger than your pop."

What goes up when the rain
comes down?

An umbrella.

What kind of animals can
jump higher than a house?

All kinds of animals. Houses
can not jump.

What holds up a train?

Bad men.

What is a bird after he is four days old?

Five days old.

What is the first thing you
put in a garden?

Your foot.

Why is an egg not like an elephant?

If you do not know, I would
not want to send you to get
eggs.

What dog keeps the best time?

A watch dog.

Why do white sheep eat so
much more than black sheep?

Because there are so many
more white sheep.

What is big and red and
eats rocks?

A big red rock eater.

How many lions can you put in an empty cage?

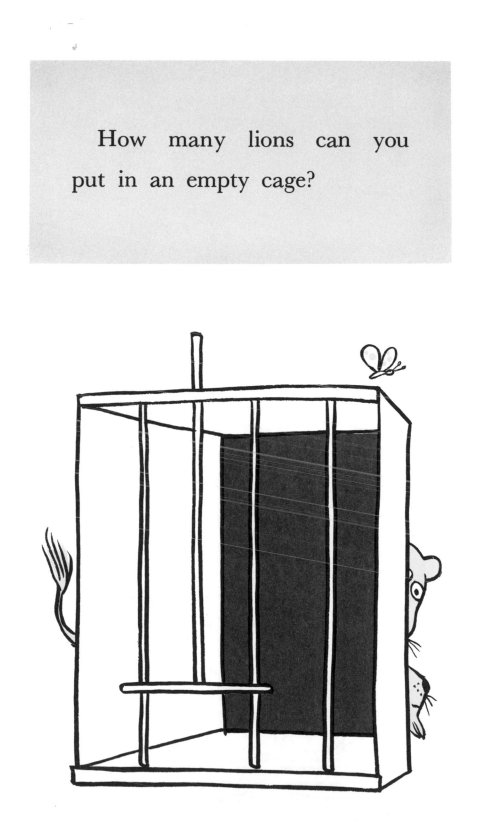

One. After that the cage is
not empty.

How many balls of string
would it take to reach the
moon?

Just one. But it would have
to be a big one.

Why does a hen lay eggs?

Because if she let them drop,
they would break.

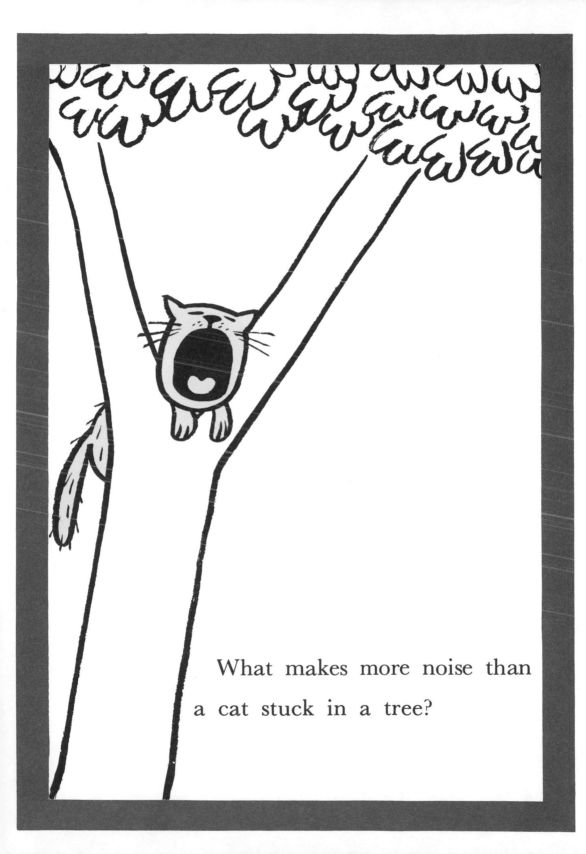

What makes more noise than
a cat stuck in a tree?

Two cats stuck in a tree.

Why does a baby pig eat so much?

To make a hog of himself.

If you drop a white hat into
the Red Sea, what will it
become?

Wet.

What kind of animal has a head like a cat and a tail like a cat, but is not a cat?

A kitten.

Why does a stork stand on
one leg?

Because if he took two legs
off the ground, he would fall
down.

Name five things that have milk in them.

Butter.

Cheese.

Ice Cream.

And two cows.

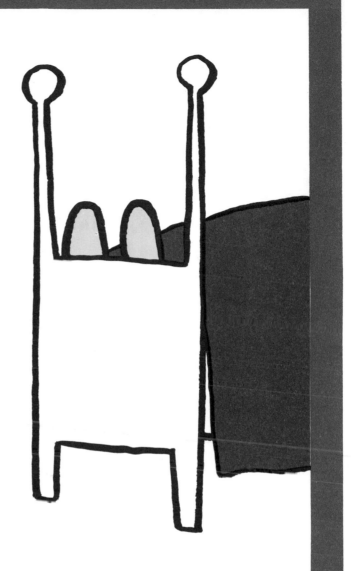

Who always goes to bed
with his shoes on?

A horse.

When is a cook bad?

When he beats an egg.

What did the pig say when
a man got him by the tail?

The pig said, "This is the
end of me."